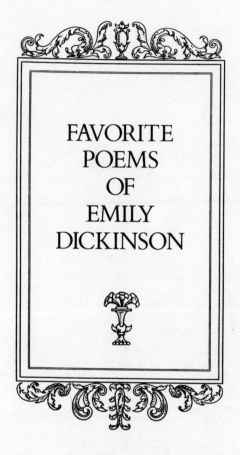

FAVORITE POEMS OF EMILY DICKINSON

Edited by two of her friends
MABEL LOOMIS TODD *and* T. W. HIGGINSON

Introduction by
CARY WILKINS

AVENEL BOOKS
New York

Originally published in 1890 as *Poems*.
Poems, Second Series was published in 1891.
Special material copyright © MCMLXXVIII
by Crown Publishers, Inc.
All rights reserved.

This edition is published by Avenel Books,
distributed by Crown Publishers, Inc.,
225 Park Avenue South, New York, New York 10003

Printed and Bound in the United States of America

Library of Congress Cataloging in Publication Data
Dickinson, Emily, 1830–1886.
    Favorite Poems of Emily Dickinson
    I. Todd, Mabel Loomis, 1856–1932.   2. Higginson,
Thomas Wentworth, 1823–1911.
PS1541.P6   1978   811'.4   78-19153

ISBN 0-517-63751-0

h g f e d c b

INTRODUCTION

---◦◦◦---

"Nobody, not even the rain, has such small hands."

Tennessee Williams used these words of E.E. Cummings as an epigraph to his play *The Glass Menagerie*. They describe the character of Laura Wingfield, a shy, reclusive girl who lives in her own private world. They are also a perfect description of Emily Dickinson, one of the most important poets in American literature.

Even though we cannot see a drop of rain filtering through the soil, we know that it may eventually supply nourishment to a seed, which will take root and blossom. But only a very few people knew about the seeds of ideas that were nourished by the unseen hands of Emily Dickinson. The hundreds of poems that blossomed from her pen were discovered—by her astonished sister—not until after her death in 1886.

Born on December 10, 1830, she spent most of her life in Amherst, Massachusetts. A school friend recalled that, although Emily was shy and retiring, there was no indication of her future reclusive life. She began writing poems in the 1850s, and her creative activity reached a peak in 1862. After that year, she withdrew more and more into herself and eventually did not even go out of the house.

It is therefore surprising to read her "letter to the world"—a treasury of poems that expands one's comprehension of life, love, nature, and immortality. Through her keen observation of people and things around her and through her deeply introspective nature, she was able to write about universal themes and feelings.

She dealt with these themes in several different ways. Casual readers of Emily Dickinson are probably familiar with only one or two sides of her personality. "If I can stop one heart from breaking" is one poem that is often associated with her. Or one may know her cute and impish side: "I'm nobody! Who are you?" She could also write, however, a poem as striking and penetrating as Ingmar

Bergman's best films: "There's a certain slant of light,/On winter afternoons." In her poem "The bustle in a house," she uses the most unusual, yet the most appropriate, images to show how death affects one: "The sweeping up the heart/And putting love away . . .." The images of violence and death in the poem "Two swimmers wrestled on the spar" are not what some people would expect from the "belle of Amherst."

She dared to break away from conventional poetic techniques by experimenting with unusual rhythms and near-rhymes. Her ability to pare a phrase to its essence is what makes her best poems so startlingly alive. Her originality makes them fresh, even after all these years.

"If fame belonged to me, I could not escape her; if she did not, the longest day would pass me on the chase, and the approbation of my dog would forsake me then." These words appear in a letter to Thomas Wentworth Higginson, one of the first editors of her poems, and explain why she did not want her poems published. "How dreary to be somebody! How public, like a frog . . .."

In addition to Mr. Higginson, she corresponded with a few close friends, "Hills . . . and the sundown, and a dog large as myself . . ."—these were the only companions she desired.

Mr. Higginson and Mabel Loomis Todd took on the job of editing her poems after her death. The first volume appeared in 1890 and is reprinted here in its entirety. Six poems from the second volume are also included. Gradually, she became recognized as an important voice in American literature, and all her poems and letters were eventually published.

Emily Dickinson dedicated herself to telling "The simple news that Nature told." One can describe her poetic gift with the words of E. E. Cummings, just as she described the mysteries of Nature with these words: "Her message is committed/To hands I cannot see . . .."

CARY WILKINS
May 1978

CONTENTS.

———◦∞◦———

		PAGE
PREFACE	. . . .	13
PRELUDE	. . . .	17

BOOK I. — LIFE.

I.	Success	19
II.	"Our share of night to bear"	20
III.	Rouge et Noir	21
IV.	Rouge gagne	22
V.	"Glee ! the great storm is over"	23
VI.	"If I can stop one heart from breaking" . . .	24
VII.	Almost	25
VIII.	"A wounded deer leaps highest"	26
IX.	"The heart asks pleasure first"	27
X.	In a Library	28
XI.	"Much madness is divinest sense"	30
XII.	"I asked no other thing"	31

CONTENTS.

		PAGE
XIII.	Exclusion	32
XIV.	The Secret	33
XV.	The Lonely House	34
XVI.	"To fight aloud is very brave"	36
XVII.	Dawn	37
XVIII.	The Book of Martyrs	38
XIX.	The Mystery of Pain	39
XX.	"I taste a liquor never brewed"	40
XXI.	A Book	41
XXII.	"I had no time to hate, because"	42
XXIII.	Unreturning	43
XXIV.	"Whether my bark went down at sea"	44
XXV.	"Belshazzar had a letter"	45
XXVI.	"The brain within its groove"	46

BOOK II. — LOVE.

		PAGE
I.	Mine	47
II.	Bequest	48
III.	"Alter? When the hills do"	49
IV.	Suspense	50
V.	Surrender	51
VI.	"If you were coming in the fall"	52
VII.	With a Flower	54

CONTENTS.

		PAGE
VIII.	Proof	55
IX.	" Have you got a brook in your little heart ? "	56
X.	Transplanted	57
XI.	The Outlet	58
XII.	In vain	59
XIII.	Renunciation	62
XIV.	Love's Baptism	64
XV.	Resurrection	66
XVI.	Apocalypse	67
XVII.	The Wife	68
XVIII.	Apotheosis	69

BOOK III. — NATURE.

I.	" New feet within my garden go "	71
II.	Mayflower	72
III.	Why ?	73
IV.	" Perhaps you 'd like to buy a flower "	74
V.	" The pedigree of honey "	75
VI.	A Service of Song	76
VII.	" The bee is not afraid of me "	77
VIII.	Summer's Armies	78
IX.	The Grass	80

CONTENTS.

		PAGE
X.	"A little road not made of man"	82
XI.	Summer Shower	83
XII.	Psalm of the Day	84
XIII.	The Sea of Sunset	86
XIV.	Purple Clover	87
XV.	The Bee	89
XVI.	"Presentiment is that long shadow"	90
XVII.	"As children bid the guest good-night"	91
XVIII.	"Angels in the early morning"	92
XIX.	"So bashful when I spied her"	93
XX.	Two Worlds	94
XXI.	The Mountain	95
XXII.	A Day	96
XXIII.	"The butterfly's assumption-gown"	97
XXIV.	The Wind	98
XXV.	Death and Life	100
XXVI.	"'T was later when the summer went"	101
XXVII.	Indian Summer	102
XXVIII.	Autumn	104
XXIX.	Beclouded	105
XXX.	The Hemlock	106
XXXI.	"There's a certain slant of light"	108

CONTENTS.

BOOK IV. — TIME AND ETERNITY.

PAGE

I. "One dignity delays for all" 109

II. Too late 110

III. Astra Castra 112

IV. "Safe in their alabaster chambers" . . . 113

V. "On this long storm the rainbow rose" . . 114

VI. From the chrysalis 115

VII. Setting sail 116

VIII. "Look back on time with kindly eyes" . . 117

IX. "A train went through a burial gate" . . 118

X. "I died for beauty, but was scarce" . . . 119

XI. Troubled about many things 120

XII. Real 121

XIII. A Funeral 122

XIV. "I went to thank her" 123

XV. "I've seen a dying eye" 124

XVI. Refuge 125

XVII. "I never saw a moor" 126

XVIII. Playmates 127

XIX. "To know just how he suffered" . . . 128

XX. "The last night that she lived" 130

CONTENTS.

		PAGE
XXI.	The First Lesson	132
XXII.	"The bustle in a house"	133
XXIII.	"I reason, earth is short"	134
XXIV.	"Afraid? Of whom am I afraid?"	135
XXV.	Dying	136
XXVI.	"Two swimmers wrestled on a spar"	137
XXVII.	The Chariot	138
XXVIII.	"She went as quiet as the dew"	140
XXIX.	Resurgam	141
XXX.	"Except to heaven she is nought"	142
XXXI.	"Death is a dialogue between"	143
XXXII.	"It was too late for man"	144
XXXIII.	Along the Potomac	145
XXXIV.	"The daisy follows soft the Sun"	146
XXXV.	Emancipation	147
XXXVI.	Lost	148
XXXVII.	"If I should n't be alive"	149
XXXVIII.	"Sleep is supposed to be"	150
XXXIX.	"I shall know why when time is over"	151
XL.	"I never lost as much but twice"	152

PREFACE.

————◦◦◦————

THE verses of Emily Dickinson belong emphatically to what Emerson long since called "the Poetry of the Portfolio," — something produced absolutely without the thought of publication, and solely by way of expression of the writer's own mind. Such verse must inevitably forfeit whatever advantage lies in the discipline of public criticism and the enforced conformity to accepted ways. On the other hand, it may often gain something through the habit of freedom and the unconventional utterance of daring thoughts. In the case of the present author, there was absolutely no choice in the matter; she must write thus, or not at all. A recluse by temperament and habit, literally spending years without setting her foot beyond the doorstep, and many more years during which her walks were strictly limited to her father's grounds, she habitually concealed her mind, like her person, from all but a very few friends; and it was with great difficulty that she was persuaded to print, during her lifetime, three or four poems. Yet she wrote verses in great abundance; and though curiously indifferent to all conventional rules, had yet a rigorous literary standard of her own, and often altered a word many times to suit an ear which had its own tenacious fastidiousness.

Miss Dickinson was born in Amherst, Mass., Dec. 10, 1830, and died there May 15, 1886. Her father, Hon. Edward Dickinson, was the leading lawyer of Amherst, and was treasurer of the well-known college there situated. It was his custom once a year to hold a large reception at his house, attended by all the families connected with the institution and by the leading people of the town. On these occasions his daughter Emily emerged from her wonted retirement and did her part as gracious hostess; nor would any one have known from her manner, I have been told, that this was not a daily occurrence. The annual occasion once past, she withdrew again into her seclusion, and except for a very few friends was as invisible to the world as if she had dwelt in a nunnery. For myself, although I had corresponded with her for many years, I saw her but twice face to face, and brought away the impression of something as unique and remote as Undine or Mignon or Thekla.

This selection from her poems is published to meet the desire of her personal friends, and especially of her surviving sister. It is believed that the thoughtful reader will find in these pages a quality more suggestive of the poetry of William Blake than of anything to be elsewhere found, — flashes of wholly original and profound insight into nature and life ; words and phrases exhibiting an extraordinary vividness of descriptive and imaginative power, yet often set in a seemingly whimsical or even rugged frame. They are here published as they were written, with very few and superficial changes ; although it is fair to say that the titles have been assigned, almost invariably, by the editors. In many cases these verses will seem to the reader like poetry torn up by the roots, with rain and

dew and earth still clinging to them, giving a fresh-
ness and a fragrance not otherwise to be conveyed.
In other cases, as in the few poems of shipwreck or
of mental conflict, we can only wonder at the gift of
vivid imagination by which this recluse woman can
delineate, by a few touches, the very crises of physical
or mental struggle. And sometimes again we catch
glimpses of a lyric strain, sustained perhaps but for a
line or two at a time, and making the reader regret its
sudden cessation. But the main quality of these
poems is that of extraordinary grasp and insight,
uttered with an uneven vigor sometimes exasperating,
seemingly wayward, but really unsought and inevitable.
After all, when a thought takes one's breath away,
a lesson on grammar seems an impertinence. As
Ruskin wrote in his earlier and better days, " No
weight nor mass nor beauty of execution can out-
weigh one grain or fragment of thought."

THOMAS WENTWORTH HIGGINSON.

THIS is my letter to the world,
  That never wrote to me, —
The simple news that Nature told,
  With tender majesty.

Her message is committed
  To hands I cannot see;
For love of her, sweet countrymen,
  judge tenderly of me!

BOOK I.

LIFE.

———◦◦◦———

I.

SUCCESS.

[Published in "A Masque of Poets" at the request of "H. H.," the author's fellow-townswoman and friend.]

SUCCESS is counted sweetest
By those who ne'er succeed.
To comprehend a nectar
Requires sorest need.

Not one of all the purple host
Who took the flag to-day
Can tell the definition,
So clear, of victory,

As he, defeated, dying,
On whose forbidden ear
The distant strains of triumph
Break, agonized and clear.

II.

OUR share of night to bear,
    Our share of morning,
Our blank in bliss to fill,
Our blank in scorning.

Here a star, and there a star,
Some lose their way.
Here a mist, and there a mist,
Afterwards — day !

III.

ROUGE ET NOIR.

SOUL, wilt thou toss again?
　　By just such a hazard
Hundreds have lost, indeed,
But tens have won an all.

Angels' breathless ballot
Lingers to record thee;
Imps in eager caucus
Raffle for my soul.

IV.

ROUGE GAGNE.

'T IS so much joy !   'T is so much joy !
    If I should fail, what poverty !
And yet, as poor as I
Have ventured all upon a throw ;
Have gained !   Yes !   Hesitated so
This side the victory !

Life is but life, and death but death !
Bliss is but bliss, and breath but breath !
And if, indeed, I fail,
At least to know the worst is sweet.
Defeat means nothing but defeat,
No drearier can prevail !

And if I gain, — oh, gun at sea,
Oh, bells that in the steeples be,
At first repeat it slow !
For heaven is a different thing
Conjectured, and waked sudden in,
And might o'erwhelm me so !

V.

G LEE ! the great storm is over !
　　Four have recovered the land ;
Forty gone down together
Into the boiling sand.

Ring, for the scant salvation !
Toll, for the bonnie souls, —
Neighbor and friend and bridegroom,
Spinning upon the shoals !

How they will tell the shipwreck
When winter shakes the door,
Till the children ask, " But the forty?
Did they come back no more? "

Then a silence suffuses the story,
And a softness the teller's eye ;
And the children no further question,
And only the waves reply.

VI.

IF I can stop one heart from breaking,
    I shall not live in vain ;
If I can ease one life the aching,
Or cool one pain,
Or help one fainting robin
Unto his nest again,
I shall not live in vain.

VII.

ALMOST!

WITHIN my reach!
　　I could have touched!
I might have chanced that way!
Soft sauntered through the village,
Sauntered as soft away!
So unsuspected violets
Within the fields lie low,
Too late for striving fingers
That passed, an hour ago.

VIII.

A WOUNDED deer leaps highest,
  I 've heard the hunter tell;
'T is but the ecstasy of death,
And then the brake is still.

The smitten rock that gushes,
The trampled steel that springs.
A cheek is always redder
Just where the hectic stings !

Mirth is the mail of anguish,
In which it cautious arm,
Lest anybody spy the blood
And " You 're hurt " exclaim !

IX.

THE heart asks pleasure first,
　　And then, excuse from pain;
And then, those little anodynes
That deaden suffering;

And then, to go to sleep;
And then, if it should be
The will of its Inquisitor,
The liberty to die.

X.

IN A LIBRARY.

A PRECIOUS, mouldering pleasure 't is
  To meet an antique book,
In just the dress his century wore ;
A privilege, I think,

His venerable hand to take,
And warming in our own,
A passage back, or two, to make
To times when he was young.

His quaint opinions to inspect,
His knowledge to unfold
On what concerns our mutual mind,
The literature of old ;

What interested scholars most,
What competitions ran
When Plato was a certainty,
And Sophocles a man ;

When Sappho was a living girl,
And Beatrice wore
The gown that Dante deified.
Facts, centuries before,

He traverses familiar,
As one should come to town
And tell you all your dreams were true :
He lived where dreams were sown.

His presence is enchantment,
You beg him not to go ;
Old volumes shake their vellum heads
And tantalize, just so.

XI.

MUCH madness is divinest sense
        To a discerning eye ;
Much sense the starkest madness.
’T is the majority
In this, as all, prevails.
Assent, and you are sane ;
Demur, — you ’re straightway dangerous,
And handled with a chain.

XII.

I ASKED no other thing,
  No other was denied.
I offered Being for it ;
The mighty merchant smiled.

Brazil? He twirled a button,
Without a glance my way :
" But, madam, is there nothing else
That we can show to-day? "

XIII.

EXCLUSION.

THE soul selects her own society,
    Then shuts the door;
On her divine majority
Obtrude no more.

Unmoved, she notes the chariot's pausing
At her low gate;
Unmoved, an emperor is kneeling
Upon her mat.

I 've known her from an ample nation
Choose one;
Then close the valves of her attention
Like stone.

XIV.

THE SECRET.

SOME things that fly there be, —
　　Birds, hours, the bumble-bee:
Of these no elegy.

Some things that stay there be, —
Grief, hills, eternity:
Nor this behooveth me.

There are, that resting, rise.
Can I expound the skies?
How still the riddle lies!

XV.

THE LONELY HOUSE.

I KNOW some lonely houses off the road
  A robber 'd like the look of. —
Wooden barred,
And windows hanging low,
Inviting to
A portico,
Where two could creep:
One hand the tools,
The other peep
To make sure all 's asleep.
Old-fashioned eyes,
Not easy to surprise !

How orderly the kitchen 'd look by night,
With just a clock, —
But they could gag the tick,
And mice won't bark ;
And so the walls don't tell,
None will.

A pair of spectacles ajar just stir —
An almanac 's aware.
Was it the mat winked,
Or a nervous star?
The moon slides down the stair
To see who 's there.

There 's plunder, — where?
Tankard, or spoon,
Earring, or stone,
A watch, some ancient brooch
To match the grandmamma,
Staid sleeping there.

Day rattles, too,
Stealth 's slow;
The sun has got as far
As the third sycamore.
Screams chanticleer,
"Who 's there?"
And echoes, trains away,
Sneer — "Where?"
While the old couple, just astir,
Fancy the sunrise left the door ajar!

XVI.

TO fight aloud is very brave,
　　But gallanter, I know,
Who charge within the bosom,
The cavalry of woe.

Who win, and nations do not see,
Who fall, and none observe,
Whose dying eyes no country
Regards with patriot love.

We trust, in plumed procession,
For such the angels go,
Rank after rank, with even feet
And uniforms of snow.

XVII.

DAWN.

WHEN night is almost done,
     And sunrise grows so near
That we can touch the spaces,
It 's time to smooth the hair

And get the dimples ready,
And wonder we could care
For that old faded midnight
That frightened but an hour.

XVIII.

THE BOOK OF MARTYRS.

READ, sweet, how others strove,
    Till we are stouter;
What they renounced,
Till we are less afraid;
How many times they bore
The faithful witness,
Till we are helped,
As if a kingdom cared!

Read then of faith
That shone above the fagot;
Clear strains of hymn
The river could not drown;
Brave names of men
And celestial women,
Passed out of record
Into renown!

XIX.

THE MYSTERY OF PAIN.

PAIN has an element of blank ;
  It cannot recollect
When it began, or if there were
A day when it was not.

It has no future but itself,
Its infinite realms contain
Its past, enlightened to perceive
New periods of pain.

XX.

I TASTE a liquor never brewed,
   From tankards scooped in pearl;
Not all the vats upon the Rhine
Yield such an alcohol!

Inebriate of air am I,
And debauchee of dew,
Reeling, through endless summer days,
From inns of molten blue.

When landlords turn the drunken bee
Out of the foxglove's door,
When butterflies renounce their drams,
I shall but drink the more!

Till seraphs swing their snowy hats,
And saints to windows run,
To see the little tippler
Leaning against the sun!

XXI.

A BOOK.

HE ate and drank the precious words,
　　His spirit grew robust ;
He knew no more that he was poor,
Nor that his frame was dust.
He danced along the dingy days,
And this bequest of wings
Was but a book.　What liberty
A loosened spirit brings !

XXII.

I HAD no time to hate, because
　　The grave would hinder me,
And life was not so ample I
Could finish enmity.

Nor had I time to love; but since
Some industry must be,
The little toil of love, I thought,
Was large enough for me.

XXIII.

UNRETURNING.

'TWAS such a little, little boat
     That toddled down the bay !
'T was such a gallant, gallant sea
That beckoned it away !

'T was such a greedy, greedy wave
That licked it from the coast ;
Nor ever guessed the stately sails
My little craft was lost !

XXIV.

WHETHER my bark went down at sea,
  Whether she met with gales,
Whether to isles enchanted
She bent her docile sails ;

By what mystic mooring
She is held to-day, —
This is the errand of the eye
Out upon the bay.

XXV.

BELSHAZZAR had a letter, —
  He never had but one ;
Belshazzar's correspondent
Concluded and begun
In that immortal copy
The conscience of us all
Can read without its glasses
On revelation's wall.

XXVI.

THE brain within its groove
　　Runs evenly and true;
But let a splinter swerve,
'T were easier for you
To put the water back
When floods have slit the hills,
And scooped a turnpike for themselves,
And blotted out the mills!

BOOK II.

LOVE.

I.

MINE.

MINE by the right of the white election!
　　Mine by the royal seal!
Mine by the sign in the scarlet prison
Bars cannot conceal!

Mine, here in vision and in veto!
Mine, by the grave's repeal
Titled, confirmed, — delirious charter!
Mine, while the ages steal!

II.

BEQUEST.

YOU left me, sweet, two legacies, —
    A legacy of love
A Heavenly Father would content,
Had He the offer of;

You left me boundaries of pain
Capacious as the sea,
Between eternity and time,
Your consciousness and me.

III.

ALTER? When the hills do.
  Falter? When the sun
Question if his glory
Be the perfect one.

Surfeit? When the daffodil
Doth of the dew:
Even as herself, O friend!
I will of you!

IV.

SUSPENSE.

ELYSIUM is as far as to
    The very nearest room,
If in that room a friend await
Felicity or doom.

What fortitude the soul contains,
That it can so endure
The accent of a coming foot,
The opening of a door !

V.

SURRENDER.

DOUBT me, my dim companion !
  Why, God would be content
With but a fraction of the love
Poured thee without a stint.
The whole of me, forever,
What more the woman can, —
Say quick, that I may dower thee
With last delight I own !

It cannot be my spirit,
For that was thine before ;
I ceded all of dust I knew, —
What opulence the more
Had I, a humble maiden,
Whose farthest of degree
Was that she might,
Some distant heaven,
Dwell timidly with thee !

VI.

IF you were coming in the fall,
    I 'd brush the summer by
With half a smile and half a spurn,
As housewives do a fly.

If I could see you in a year,
I 'd wind the months in balls,
And put them each in separate drawers,
Until their time befalls.

If only centuries delayed,
I 'd count them on my hand,
Subtracting till my fingers dropped
Into Van Diemen's land.

If certain, when this life was out,
That yours and mine should be,
I 'd toss it yonder like a rind,
And taste eternity.

But now, all ignorant of the length
Of time's uncertain wing,
It goads me, like the goblin bee,
That will not state its sting.

VII.

WITH A FLOWER.

I HIDE myself within my flower,
 That wearing on your breast,
You, unsuspecting, wear me too —
And angels know the rest.

I hide myself within my flower,
That, fading from your vase,
You, unsuspecting, feel for me
Almost a loneliness.

VIII.

PROOF.

THAT I did always love,
   I bring thee proof:
That till I loved
I did not love enough.

That I shall love alway,
I offer thee
That love is life,
And life hath immortality.

This, dost thou doubt, sweet?
Then have I
Nothing to show
But Calvary.

IX.

HAVE you got a brook in your little heart,
    Where bashful flowers blow,
And blushing birds go down to drink,
And shadows tremble so?

And nobody knows, so still it flows,
That any brook is there;
And yet your little draught of life
Is daily drunken there.

Then look out for the little brook in March,
When the rivers overflow,
And the snows come hurrying from the hills,
And the bridges often go.

And later, in August it may be,
When the meadows parching lie,
Beware, lest this little brook of life
Some burning noon go dry !

X.

TRANSPLANTED.

AS if some little Arctic flower,
   Upon the polar hem,
Went wandering down the latitudes,
Until it puzzled came
To continents of summer,
To firmaments of sun,
To strange, bright crowds of flowers,
And birds of foreign tongue !
I say, as if this little flower
To Eden wandered in —
What then ? Why, nothing, only
Your inference therefrom !

XI.

THE OUTLET.

M Y river runs to thee :
Blue sea, wilt welcome me?

My river waits reply.
Oh sea, look graciously !

I 'll fetch thee brooks
From spotted nooks, —

Say, sea,
Take me !

XII.

IN VAIN.

I CANNOT live with you,
   It would be life,
And life is over there
Behind the shelf

The sexton keeps the key to,
Putting up
Our life, his porcelain,
Like a cup

Discarded of the housewife,
Quaint or broken ;
A newer Sèvres pleases,
Old ones crack.

I could not die with you,
For one must wait
To shut the other's gaze down, —
You could not.

And I, could I stand by
And see you freeze,
Without my right of frost,
Death's privilege?

Nor could I rise with you,
Because your face
Would put out Jesus',
That new grace

Glow plain and foreign
On my homesick eye,
Except that you, than he
Shone closer by.

They 'd judge us — how?
For you served Heaven, you know,
Or sought to ;
I could not,

Because you saturated sight,
And I had no more eyes
For sordid excellence
As Paradise.

And were you lost, I would be,
Though my name
Rang loudest
On the heavenly fame.

And were you saved,
And I condemned to be
Where you were not,
That self were hell to me.

So we must keep apart,
You there, I here,
With just the door ajar
That oceans are,
And prayer,
And that pale sustenance,
Despair !

XIII.

RENUNCIATION.

THERE came a day at summer's full
    Entirely for me ;
I thought that such were for the saints,
Where revelations be.

The sun, as common, went abroad,
The flowers, accustomed, blew,
As if no soul the solstice passed
That maketh all things new.

The time was scarce profaned by speech ;
The symbol of a word
Was needless, as at sacrament
The wardrobe of our Lord.

Each was to each the sealed church,
Permitted to commune this time,
Lest we too awkward show
At supper of the Lamb.

The hours slid fast, as hours will,
Clutched tight by greedy hands ;
So faces on two decks look back,
Bound to opposing lands.

And so, when all the time had failed,
Without external sound,
Each bound the other's crucifix,
We gave no other bond.

Sufficient troth that we shall rise —
Deposed, at length, the grave —
To that new marriage, justified
Through Calvaries of Love !

XIV.

LOVE'S BAPTISM.

I 'M ceded, I 've stopped being theirs;
    The name they dropped upon my face
With water, in the country church,
Is finished using now,
And they can put it with my dolls,
My childhood, and the string of spools
I 've finished threading too.

Baptized before without the choice,
But this time consciously, of grace
Unto supremest name,
Called to my full, the crescent dropped,
Existence's whole arc filled up
With one small diadem.

My second rank, too small the first,
Crowned, crowing on my father's breast,

A half unconscious queen ;
But this time, adequate, erect,
With will to choose or to reject,
And I choose — just a throne.

XV.

RESURRECTION.

'TWAS a long parting, but the time
  For interview had come ;
Before the judgment-seat of God,
  The last and second time

These fleshless lovers met,
  A heaven in a gaze,
A heaven of heavens, the privilege
  Of one another's eyes.

No lifetime set on them,
  Apparelled as the new
Unborn, except they had beheld,
  Born everlasting now.

Was bridal e'er like this ?
  A paradise, the host,
And cherubim and seraphim
  The most familiar guest.

XVI.

APOCALYPSE.

I 'M wife ; I 've finished that,
    That other state ;
I 'm Czar, I 'm woman now :
It 's safer so.

How odd the girl's life looks
Behind this soft eclipse !
I think that earth seems so
To those in heaven now.

This being comfort, then
That other kind was pain ;
But why compare ?
I 'm wife ! stop there !

XVII.

THE WIFE.

SHE rose to his requirement, dropped
　　The playthings of her life
To take the honorable work
Of woman and of wife.

If aught she missed in her new day
Of amplitude, or awe,
Or first prospective, or the gold
In using wore away,

It lay unmentioned, as the sea
Develops pearl and weed,
But only to himself is known
The fathoms they abide.

XVIII.

APOTHEOSIS.

COME slowly, Eden !
    Lips unused to thee,
Bashful, sip thy jasmines,
As the fainting bee,

Reaching late his flower,
Round her chamber hums,
Counts his nectars — enters,
And is lost in balms !

BOOK III.
NATURE.

NEW feet within my garden go,
New fingers stir the sod;
A troubadour upon the elm
Betrays the solitude.

New children play upon the green,
New weary sleep below;
And still the pensive spring returns,
And still the punctual snow !

II.

MAY-FLOWER.

PINK, small, and punctual.
　　Aromatic, low,
Covert in April,
Candid in May,

Dear to the moss,
Known by the knoll,
Next to the robin
In every human soul.

Bold little beauty,
Bedecked with thee.
Nature forswears
Antiquity.

III.

WHY?

THE murmur of a bee
    A witchcraft yieldeth me.
If any ask me why,
'T were easier to die
Than tell.

The red upon the hill
Taketh away my will;
If anybody sneer,
Take care, for God is here,
That 's all.

The breaking of the day
Addeth to my degree;
If any ask me how,
Artist, who drew me so,
Must tell !

IV.

PERHAPS you 'd like to buy a flower?
But I could never sell.
If you would like to borrow
Until the daffodil

Unties her yellow bonnet
Beneath the village door,
Until the bees, from clover rows
Their hock and sherry draw,

Why, I will lend until just then,
But not an hour more !

V.

THE pedigree of honey
    Does not concern the bee ;
A clover, any time, to him
Is aristocracy.

VI.

A SERVICE OF SONG.

SOME keep the Sabbath going to church;
  I keep it staying at home,
With a bobolink for a chorister,
And an orchard for a dome.

Some keep the Sabbath in surplice;
I just wear my wings,
And instead of tolling the bell for church,
Our little sexton sings.

God preaches, — a noted clergyman, —
And the sermon is never long;
So instead of getting to heaven at last,
I 'm going all along!

VII.

THE bee is not afraid of me,
    I know the butterfly;
The pretty people in the woods
Receive me cordially.

The brooks laugh louder when I come,
The breezes madder play.
Wherefore, mine eyes, thy silver mists?
Wherefore, O summer's day?

VIII.

SUMMER'S ARMIES.

SOME rainbow coming from the fair !
Some vision of the world Cashmere
I confidently see !
Or else a peacock's purple train,
Feather by feather, on the plain
Fritters itself away !

The dreamy butterflies bestir,
Lethargic pools resume the whir
Of last year's sundered tune.
From some old fortress on the sun
Baronial bees march, one by one,
In murmuring platoon !

The robins stand as thick to-day
As flakes of snow stood yesterday,

On fence and roof and twig.
The orchis binds her feather on
For her old lover, Don the Sun,
Revisiting the bog !

Without commander, countless, still,
The regiment of wood and hill
In bright detachment stand.
Behold !   Whose multitudes are these?
The children of whose turbaned seas,
Or what Circassian land?

IX.

THE GRASS.

THE grass so little has to do, —
    A sphere of simple green,
With only butterflies to brood,
And bees to entertain,

And stir all day to pretty tunes
The breezes fetch along,
And hold the sunshine in its lap
And bow to everything;

And thread the dews all night, like pearls,
And make itself so fine, —
A duchess were too common
For such a noticing.

And even when it dies, to pass
In odors so divine,
As lowly spices gone to sleep,
Or amulets of pine.

And then to dwell in sovereign barns,
And dream the days away, —
The grass so little has to do,
I wish I were the hay!

X.

A LITTLE road not made of man,
　　Enabled of the eye,
Accessible to thill of bee,
Or cart of butterfly.

If town it have, beyond itself,
'T is that I cannot say ;
I only sigh, — no vehicle
Bears me along that way.

XI.

SUMMER SHOWER.

A DROP fell on the apple-tree,
    Another on the roof;
A half a dozen kissed the eaves,
And made the gables laugh.

A few went out to help the brook,
That went to help the sea.
Myself conjectured, Were they pearls,
What necklaces could be !

The dust replaced in hoisted roads,
The birds jocoser sung ;
The sunshine threw his hat away,
The orchards spangles hung.

The breezes brought dejected lutes,
And bathed them in the glee ;
The East put out a single flag,
And signed the fête away.

XII.

PSALM OF THE DAY.

A SOMETHING in a summer's day,
    As slow her flambeaux burn away,
Which solemnizes me.

A something in a summer's noon, —
An azure depth, a wordless tune,
Transcending ecstasy.

And still within a summer's night
A something so transporting bright,
I clap my hands to see ;

Then veil my too inspecting face,
Lest such a subtle, shimmering grace
Flutter too far for me.

The wizard-fingers never rest,
The purple brook within the breast
Still chafes its narrow bed ;

Still rears the East her amber flag,
Guides still the sun along the crag
His caravan of red,

Like flowers that heard the tale of dews,
But never deemed the dripping prize
Awaited their low brows;

Or bees, that thought the summer's name
Some rumor of delirium
No summer could for them;

Or Arctic creature, dimly stirred
By tropic hint, — some travelled bird
Imported to the wood;

Or wind's bright signal to the ear,
Making that homely and severe,
Contented, known, before

The heaven unexpected came,
To lives that thought their worshipping
A too presumptuous psalm.

XIII.

THE SEA OF SUNSET.

THIS is the land the sunset washes,
　　These are the banks of the Yellow Sea ;
Where it rose, or whither it rushes,
These are the western mystery !

Night after night her purple traffic
Strews the landing with opal bales ;
Merchantmen poise upon horizons,
Dip, and vanish with fairy sails.

XIV.

PURPLE CLOVER.

THERE is a flower that bees prefer,
    And butterflies desire ;
To gain the purple democrat
The humming-birds aspire.

And whatsoever insect pass,
A honey bears away
Proportioned to his several dearth
And her capacity.

Her face is rounder than the moon,
And ruddier than the gown
Of orchis in the pasture,
Or rhododendron worn.

She doth not wait for June ;
Before the world is green
Her sturdy little countenance
Against the wind is seen,

Contending with the grass,
Near kinsman to herself,
For privilege of sod and sun,
Sweet litigants for life.

And when the hills are full,
And newer fashions blow,
Doth not retract a single spice
For pang of jealousy.

Her public is the noon,
Her providence the sun,
Her progress by the bee proclaimed
In sovereign, swerveless tune.

The bravest of the host,
Surrendering the last,
Nor even of defeat aware
When cancelled by the frost.

XV.

THE BEE.

L IKE trains of cars on tracks of plush
I hear the level bee :
A jar across the flowers goes,
Their velvet masonry

Withstands until the sweet assault
Their chivalry consumes,
While he, victorious, tilts away
To vanquish other blooms.

His feet are shod with gauze,
His helmet is of gold ;
His breast, a single onyx
With chrysoprase, inlaid.

His labor is a chant,
His idleness a tune ;
Oh, for a bee's experience
Of clovers and of noon !

XVI.

PRESENTIMENT is that long shadow on the lawn
    Indicative that suns go down ;
The notice to the startled grass
That darkness is about to pass.

XVII.

AS children bid the guest good-night,
And then reluctant turn,
My flowers raise their pretty lips,
Then put their nightgowns on.

As children caper when they wake,
Merry that it is morn,
My flowers from a hundred cribs
Will peep, and prance again.

XVIII.

A NGELS in the early morning
　　May be seen the dews among,
Stooping, plucking, smiling, flying :
Do the buds to them belong?

Angels when the sun is hottest
May be seen the sands among,
Stooping, plucking, sighing, flying ;
Parched the flowers they bear along.

XIX.

So bashful when I spied her,
    So pretty, so ashamed !
So hidden in her leaflets,
Lest anybody find ;

So breathless till I passed her,
So helpless when I turned
And bore her, struggling, blushing,
Her simple haunts beyond !

For whom I robbed the dingle,
For whom betrayed the dell,
Many will doubtless ask me,
But I shall never tell !

XX.

TWO WORLDS.

IT makes no difference abroad,
  The seasons fit the same,
The mornings blossom into noons,
And split their pods of flame.

Wild-flowers kindle in the woods,
The brooks brag all the day;
No blackbird bates his jargoning
For passing Calvary.

Auto-da-fé and judgment
Are nothing to the bee;
His separation from his rose
To him seems misery.

XXI.

THE MOUNTAIN.

THE mountain sat upon the plain
      In his eternal chair,
His observation omnifold,
His inquest everywhere.

The seasons prayed around his knees,
Like children round a sire :
Grandfather of the days is he,
Of dawn the ancestor.

XXII.

A DAY.

I 'LL tell you how the sun rose, —
  A ribbon at a time.
The steeples swam in amethyst,
The news like squirrels ran.

The hills untied their bonnets,
The bobolinks begun.
Then I said softly to myself,
"That must have been the sun!"

. . . . . .

But how he set, I know not.
There seemed a purple stile
Which little yellow boys and girls
Were climbing all the while

Till when they reached the other side,
A dominie in gray
Put gently up the evening bars,
And led the flock away.

XXIII.

THE butterfly's assumption-gown,
　　In chrysoprase apartments hung,
This afternoon put on.

How condescending to descend,
And be of buttercups the friend
　　In a New England town!

XXIV.

THE WIND.

OF all the sounds despatched abroad,
  There 's not a charge to me
Like that old measure in the boughs,
That phraseless melody

The wind does, working like a hand
Whose fingers brush the sky,
Then quiver down, with tufts of tune
Permitted gods and me.

When winds go round and round in bands,
And thrum upon the door,
And birds take places overhead,
To bear them orchestra,

I crave him grace, of summer boughs,
If such an outcast be,
He never heard that fleshless chant
Rise solemn in the tree,

As if some caravan of sound
On deserts, in the sky,
Had broken rank,
Then knit, and passed
In seamless company.

XXV.

DEATH AND LIFE.

APPARENTLY with no surprise
  To any happy flower,
The frost beheads it at its play
In accidental power.
The blond assassin passes on,
The sun proceeds unmoved
To measure off another day
For an approving God.

XXVI.

'TWAS later when the summer went
　　Than when the cricket came,
And yet we knew that gentle clock
Meant nought but going home.

'T was sooner when the cricket went
Than when the winter came,
Yet that pathetic pendulum
Keeps esoteric time.

XXVII.

INDIAN SUMMER.

THESE are the days when birds come back,
  A very few, a bird or two,
To take a backward look.

These are the days when skies put on
The old, old sophistries of June, —
A blue and gold mistake.

Oh, fraud that cannot cheat the bee,
Almost thy plausibility
Induces my belief,

Till ranks of seeds their witness bear,
And softly through the altered air
Hurries a timid leaf!

Oh, sacrament of summer days,
Oh, last communion in the haze,
Permit a child to join,

Thy sacred emblems to partake,
Thy consecrated bread to break,
Taste thine immortal wine !

XXVIII.

AUTUMN.

THE morns are meeker than they were,
    The nuts are getting brown;
The berry's cheek is plumper,
The rose is out of town.

The maple wears a gayer scarf,
The field a scarlet gown.
Lest I should be old-fashioned,
I 'll put a trinket on.

XXIX.

BECLOUDED.

THE sky is low, the clouds are mean,
   A travelling flake of snow
Across a barn or through a rut
Debates if it will go.

A narrow wind complains all day
How some one treated him ;
Nature, like us, is sometimes caught
Without her diadem.

XXX.

THE HEMLOCK.

I THINK the hemlock likes to stand
    Upon a marge of snow;
It suits his own austerity,
And satisfies an awe

That men must slake in wilderness,
Or in the desert cloy, —
An instinct for the hoar, the bald,
Lapland's necessity.

The hemlock's nature thrives on cold;
The gnash of northern winds
Is sweetest nutriment to him,
His best Norwegian wines.

To satin races he is nought ;
But children on the Don
Beneath his tabernacles play,
And Dnieper wrestlers run.

XXXI.

THERE 'S a certain slant of light,
   On winter afternoons,
That oppresses, like the weight
Of cathedral tunes.

Heavenly hurt it gives us;
We can find no scar,
But internal difference
Where the meanings are.

None may teach it anything,
' T is the seal, despair, —
An imperial affliction
Sent us of the air.

When it comes, the landscape listens,
Shadows hold their breath;
When it goes, 't is like the distance
On the look of death.

BOOK IV.

TIME AND ETERNITY.

I.

ONE dignity delays for all,
    One mitred afternoon.
None can avoid this purple,
None evade this crown.

Coach it insures, and footmen,
Chamber and state and throng;
Bells, also, in the village,
As we ride grand along.

What dignified attendants,
What service when we pause!
How loyally at parting
Their hundred hats they raise!

How pomp surpassing ermine,
When simple you and I
Present our meek escutcheon,
And claim the rank to die!

II.

TOO LATE.

DELAYED till she had ceased to know,
   Delayed till in its vest of snow
  Her loving bosom lay.
An hour behind the fleeting breath,
Later by just an hour than death, —
  Oh, lagging yesterday !

Could she have guessed that it would be ;
Could but a crier of the glee
  Have climbed the distant hill ;
Had not the bliss so slow a pace, —
Who knows but this surrendered face
  Were undefeated still ?

Oh, if there may departing be
Any forgot by victory
   In her imperial round,
Show them this meek apparelled thing,
That could not stop to be a king,
   Doubtful if it be crowned !

III.

ASTRA CASTRA.

DEPARTED to the judgment,
  A mighty afternoon;
Great clouds like ushers leaning,
Creation looking on.

The flesh surrendered, cancelled,
The bodiless begun;
Two worlds, like audiences, disperse
And leave the soul alone.

IV.

SAFE in their alabaster chambers,
    Untouched by morning and untouched by noon,
Sleep the meek members of the resurrection,
Rafter of satin, and roof of stone.

Light laughs the breeze in her castle of sunshine;
Babbles the bee in a stolid ear;
Pipe the sweet birds in ignorant cadence, —
Ah, what sagacity perished here!

Grand go the years in the crescent above them;
Worlds scoop their arcs, and firmaments row,
Diadems drop and Doges surrender,
Soundless as dots on a disk of snow.

V.

ON this long storm the rainbow rose,
    On this late morn the sun ;
The clouds, like listless elephants,
Horizons straggled down.

The birds rose smiling in their nests,
The gales indeed were done ;
Alas ! how heedless were the eyes
On whom the summer shone !

The quiet nonchalance of death
No daybreak can bestir ;
The slow archangel's syllables
Must awaken her.

VI.

FROM THE CHRYSALIS.

MY cocoon tightens, colors tease,
  I 'm feeling for the air;
A dim capacity for wings
Degrades the dress I wear.

A power of butterfly must be
The aptitude to fly,
Meadows of majesty concedes
And easy sweeps of sky.

So I must baffle at the hint
And cipher at the sign,
And make much blunder, if at last
I take the clew divine.

VII.

SETTING SAIL.

EXULTATION is the going
       Of an inland soul to sea, —
Past the houses, past the headlands,
Into deep eternity !

Bred as we, among the mountains,
Can the sailor understand
The divine intoxication
Of the first league out from land?

VIII.

LOOK back on time with kindly eyes,
    He doubtless did his best;
How softly sinks his trembling sun
In human nature's west!

IX.

A TRAIN went through a burial gate,
　　A bird broke forth and sang,
And trilled, and quivered, and shook his throat
Till all the churchyard rang ;

And then adjusted his little notes,
And bowed and sang again.
Doubtless, he thought it meet of him
To say good-by to men.

X.

I DIED for beauty, but was scarce
    Adjusted in the tomb,
When one who died for truth was lain
In an adjoining room.

He questioned softly why I failed?
" For beauty," I replied.
" And I for truth, — the two are one ;
We brethren are," he said.

And so, as kinsmen met a night,
We talked between the rooms,
Until the moss had reached our lips,
And covered up our names.

XI.

"TROUBLED ABOUT MANY THINGS."

HOW many times these low feet staggered,
   Only the soldered mouth can tell;
Try! can you stir the awful rivet?
Try! can you lift the hasps of steel?

Stroke the cool forehead, hot so often,
Lift, if you can, the listless hair;
Handle the adamantine fingers
Never a thimble more shall wear.

Buzz the dull flies on the chamber window;
Brave shines the sun through the freckled pane;
Fearless the cobweb swings from the ceiling —
Indolent housewife, in daisies lain!

XII.

REAL.

I LIKE a look of agony,
    Because I know it 's true ;
Men do not sham convulsion,
Nor simulate a throe.

The eyes glaze once, and that is death.
Impossible to feign
The beads upon the forehead
By homely anguish strung.

XIII.

THE FUNERAL.

THAT short, potential stir
    That each can make but once,
That bustle so illustrious
'T is almost consequence,

Is the *éclat* of death.
Oh, thou unknown renown
That not a beggar would accept,
Had he the power to spurn !

XIV.

I WENT to thank her,
    But she slept;
Her bed a funnelled stone,
With nosegays at the head and foot,
That travellers had thrown,

Who went to thank her;
But she slept.
'T was short to cross the sea
To look upon her like, alive,
But turning back 't was slow.

XV.

I 'VE seen a dying eye
    Run round and round a room
In search of something, as it seemed,
Then cloudier become;
And then, obscure with fog,
And then be soldered down,
Without disclosing what it be,
'T were blessed to have seen.

XVI.

REFUGE.

THE clouds their backs together laid,
    The north begun to push,
The forests galloped till they fell,
The lightning skipped like mice ;
The thunder crumbled like a stuff —
How good to be safe in tombs,
Where nature's temper cannot reach,
Nor vengeance ever comes !

XVII.

I NEVER saw a moor,
  I never saw the sea;
Yet know I how the heather looks,
And what a wave must be.

I never spoke with God,
Nor visited in heaven;
Yet certain am I of the spot
As if the chart were given.

XVIII.

PLAYMATES.

GOD permits industrious angels
　　Afternoons to play.
I met one, — forgot my school-mates,
All, for him, straightway.

God calls home the angels promptly
At the setting sun ;
I missed mine.　How dreary marbles,
After playing Crown !

XIX.

TO know just how he suffered would be dear;
　　To know if any human eyes were near
To whom he could intrust his wavering gaze,
Until it settled firm on Paradise.

To know if he was patient, part content,
Was dying as he thought, or different;
Was it a pleasant day to die,
And did the sunshine face his way?

What was his furthest mind, of home, or God,
Or what the distant say
At news that he ceased human nature
On such a day?

And wishes, had he any?
Just his sigh, accented,
Had been legible to me.
And was he confident until
Ill fluttered out in everlasting well?

And if he spoke, what name was best,
What first,
What one broke off with
At the drowsiest?

Was he afraid, or tranquil?
Might he know
How conscious consciousness could grow,
Till love that was, and love too blest to be,
Meet — and the junction be Eternity?

XX.

THE last night that she lived,
   It was a common night,
Except the dying; this to us
Made nature different.

We noticed smallest things, —
Things overlooked before,
By this great light upon our minds
Italicized, as 't were.

That others could exist
While she must finish quite,
A jealousy for her arose
So nearly infinite.

We waited while she passed;
It was a narrow time,
Too jostled were our souls to speak,
At length the notice came.

She mentioned, and forgot;
Then lightly as a reed
Bent to the water, shivered scarce,
Consented, and was dead.

And we, we placed the hair,
And drew the head erect;
And then an awful leisure was,
Our faith to regulate.

XXI.

THE FIRST LESSON.

NOT in this world to see his face
　　Sounds long, until I read the place
Where this is said to be
But just the primer to a life
Unopened, rare, upon the shelf,
Clasped yet to him and me.

And yet, my primer suits me so
I would not choose a book to know
Than that, be sweeter wise ;
Might some one else so learned be,
And leave me just my A B C,
Himself could have the skies.

XXII.

THE bustle in a house
    The morning after death
Is solemnest of industries
Enacted upon earth, —

The sweeping up the heart,
And putting love away
We shall not want to use again
Until eternity.

XXIII.

I REASON, earth is short,
    And anguish absolute.
And many hurt ;
But what of that ?

I reason, we could die :
The best vitality
Cannot excel decay ;
But what of that ?

I reason that in heaven
Somehow, it will be even,
Some new equation given
But what of that ?

XXIV.

AFRAID? Of whom am I afraid?
　　Not death; for who is he?
The porter of my father's lodge
As much abasheth me.

Of life? 'T were odd I fear a thing
That comprehendeth me
In one or more existences
At Deity's decree.

Of resurrection? Is the east
Afraid to trust the morn
With her fastidious forehead?
As soon impeach my crown!

XXV.

DYING.

THE sun kept setting, setting still;
    No hue of afternoon
Upon the village I perceived, —
From house to house 't was noon.

The dusk kept dropping, dropping still;
No dew upon the grass,
But only on my forehead stopped,
And wandered in my face.

My feet kept drowsing, drowsing still,
My fingers were awake;
Yet why so little sound myself
Unto my seeming make?

How well I knew the light before!
I could not see it now.
'T is dying, I am doing; but
I 'm not afraid to know.

XXVI.

TWO swimmers wrestled on the spar
    Until the morning sun,
When one turned smiling to the land.
O God, the other one !

The stray ships passing spied a face
Upon the waters borne,
With eyes in death still begging raised,
And hands beseeching thrown.

XXVII.

THE CHARIOT.

BECAUSE I could not stop for Death,
    He kindly stopped for me;
The carriage held but just ourselves
And Immortality.

We slowly drove, he knew no haste,
And I had put away
My labor, and my leisure too,
For his civility.

We passed the school where children played,
Their lessons scarcely done;
We passed the fields of gazing grain,
We passed the setting sun.

We paused before a house that seemed
A swelling of the ground ;
The roof was scarcely visible,
The cornice but a mound.

Since then 't is centuries ; but each
Feels shorter than the day
I first surmised the horses' heads
Were toward eternity.

XXVIII.

SHE went as quiet as the dew
    From a familiar flower.
Not like the dew did she return
At the accustomed hour!

She dropt as softly as a star
From out my summer's eve;
Less skilful than Leverrier
It 's sorer to believe!

XXIX.

RESURGAM.

AT last to be identified !
    At last, the lamps upon thy side,
The rest of life to see !
Past midnight, past the morning star !
Past sunrise ! Ah ! what leagues there are
Between our feet and day !

XXX.

EXCEPT to heaven, she is nought;
　　Except for angels, lone;
Except to some wide-wandering bee,
A flower superfluous blown;

Except for winds, provincial;
Except by butterflies,
Unnoticed as a single dew
That on the acre lies.

The smallest housewife in the grass,
Yet take her from the lawn,
And somebody has lost the face
That made existence home!

XXXI.

DEATH is a dialogue between
The spirit and the dust.
" Dissolve," says Death. The Spirit, " Sir,
I have another trust."

Death doubts it, argues from the ground.
The Spirit turns away,
Just laying off, for evidence,
An overcoat of clay.

XXXII.

I T was too late for man,
    But early yet for God;
Creation impotent to help,
But prayer remained our side.

How excellent the heaven,
When earth cannot be had;
How hospitable, then, the face
Of our old neighbor, God!

XXXIII.

ALONG THE POTOMAC.

WHEN I was small, a woman died.
    To-day her only boy
Went up from the Potomac,
His face all victory,

To look at her; how slowly
The seasons must have turned
Till bullets clipt an angle,
And he passed quickly round!

If pride shall be in Paradise
I never can decide;
Of their imperial conduct,
No person testified.

But proud in apparition,
That woman and her boy
Pass back and forth before my brain,
As ever in the sky.

XXXIV.

THE daisy follows soft the sun,
    And when his golden walk is done,
Sits shyly at his feet.
He, waking, finds the flower near.
" Wherefore, marauder, art thou here?
    " Because, sir, love is sweet ! "

We are the flower, Thou the sun !
Forgive us, if as days decline,
    We nearer steal to Thee, —
Enamoured of the parting west,
The peace, the flight, the amethyst,
    Night's possibility !

XXXV.

EMANCIPATION.

NO rack can torture me,
  My soul 's at liberty.
Behind this mortal bone
There knits a bolder one

You cannot prick with saw,
Nor rend with scymitar.
Two bodies therefore be ;
Bind one, and one will flee.

The eagle of his nest
No easier divest
And gain the sky,
Than mayest thou,

Except thyself may be
Thine enemy ;
Captivity is consciousness,
So 's liberty.

XXXVI.

LOST.

I LOST a world the other day.
　　Has anybody found?
You 'll know it by the row of stars
Around its forehead bound.

A rich man might not notice it;
Yet to my frugal eye
Of more esteem than ducats.
Oh, find it, sir, for me!

XXXVII.

I F I should n't be alive
        When the robins come,
Give the one in red cravat
A memorial crumb.

If I could n't thank you,
Being just asleep,
You will know I 'm trying
With my granite lip !

XXXVIII.

SLEEP is supposed to be,
    By souls of sanity,
The shutting of the eye.

Sleep is the station grand
Down which on either hand
The hosts of witness stand !

Morn is supposed to be,
By people of degree,
The breaking of the day.

Morning has not occurred !
That shall aurora be
East of eternity ;

One with the banner gay,
One in the red array, —
That is the break of day.

XXXIX.

I SHALL know why, when time is over,
  And I have ceased to wonder why;
Christ will explain each separate anguish
In the fair schoolroom of the sky.

He will tell me what Peter promised,
And I, for wonder at his woe,
I shall forget the drop of anguish
That scalds me now, that scalds me now.

XL.

I NEVER lost as much but twice,
    And that was in the sod ;
Twice have I stood a beggar
Before the door of God !

Angels, twice descending,
Reimbursed my store.
Burglar, banker, father,
I am poor once more !

Selections from

POEMS, SECOND SERIES

———◦◦———

This selection is taken from the second volume of Emily Dickinson's poems, which was
also edited by Mabel Loomis Todd and
Thomas Wentworth Higginson.

I'm nobody! Who are you?
Are you nobody, too?
Then there's a pair of us—don't tell!
They'd banish us, you know.

How dreary to be somebody!
How public, like a frog
To tell your name the livelong day
To an admiring bog!

THE WHITE HEAT

Dare you see a soul at the white heat?
   Then crouch within the door.
Red is the fire's common tint;
   But when the vivid ore

Has sated flame's conditions,
   Its quivering substance plays
Without a color but the light
   Of unanointed blaze.

Least village boasts its blacksmith,
   Whose anvil's even din
Stands symbol for the finer forge
   That soundless tugs within,

Refining these impatient ores
   With hammer and with blaze,
Until the designated light
   Repudiate the forge.

APRIL

An altered look about the hills;
A Tyrian light the village fills;
A wider sunrise in the dawn;
A deeper twilight on the lawn;
A print of a vermilion foot;
A purple finger on the slope;
A flippant fly upon the pane;
A spider at his trade again;
An added strut in chanticleer;
A flower expected everywhere;
An axe shrill singing in the woods;
Fern-odors on untravelled roads,—
All this, and more I cannot tell,
A furtive look you know as well,
And Nicodemus' mystery
Receives its annual reply.

THE SNAKE

A narrow fellow in the grass
Occasionally rides;
You may have met him,—did you not,
His notice sudden is.

The grass divides as with a comb,
A spotted shaft is seen;
And then it closes at your feet
And opens further on.

He likes a boggy acre,
A floor too cool for corn.
Yet when a child, and barefoot,
I more than once, at morn,

Have passed, I thought, a whip-lash
Unbraiding in the sun,—
When, stooping to secure it,
It wrinkled, and was gone.

Several of nature's people
I know, and they know me;
I feel for them a transport
Of cordiality;

But never met this fellow,
Attended or alone,
Without a tighter breathing,
And zero at the bone.

THE HUMMING-BIRD

A route of evanescence
With a revolving wheel;
A resonance of emerald,
A rush of cochineal;
And every blossom on the bush
Adjusts its tumbled head,—
The mail from Tunis, probably,
An easy morning's ride.

As imperceptibly as grief
The summer lapsed away,—
Too imperceptible, at last,
To seem like perfidy.

A quietness distilled,
As twilight long begun,
Or Nature, spending with herself
Sequestered afternoon.

The dusk drew earlier in
The morning foreign shone,—
A courteous, yet harrowing grace,
As guest who would be gone.

And thus, without a wing,
Or service of a keel,
Our summer made her light escape
Into the beautiful.